MW01026095

Braiding Rugs

by Nancy Bubel

Why Braid Rugs?

Grandmother Stone's big braided rug in the parlor was a true conversation piece.

Matriarch of a large family, she remembered the source of each strip of wool in the rug, the person who had worn the garment first, and the person who had worn it after it had been "made over."

She could (and often did) recall exactly when the children had worn a garment ("John wore that coat when he was in the second grade. It was that very cold winter, and he had the croup.") and some incidents of that period connected with person involved. Looking at the orderly handiwork in that rug was to her like leafing through a photograph album. Each piece of cloth had its story, some humorous, some sad, with the sadness softened by the years.

Braiding rugs is an ideal hobby for men and women. There are no expensive lessons on how to braid. It is good for idle moments, and even five or ten minutes can be productive time. You have an opportunity to show your artistic talents in combining colors in intriguing patterns. You have the deep satisfaction of making something valuable from what many would call worthless rags. Remember: Waste not, want not. All this and the most practical of results, a rug that is lasting and that will win words of admiration from your family and guests.

And, if you braid in some strips from garments with memories attached, you too will braid a rug that is much more than a rug to you. Let Nancy Bubel show you how in the following pages.

The Garden Way Staff

Braiding Rugs

by
Nancy Bubel

The craft of rug braiding, like so many other good things, is rooted in necessity. Americans of an earlier day found that they could use what they had — in this case, "rags" of worn clothing, to create the rugs they needed for warmth in the drafty floors of their inefficiently heated homes.

Braided rugs have never really gone out of "style" (whatever that is!), but today there are more reasons that ever for using this time-honored craft to produce the rugs we need for our homes.

* Anyone can do it. Braiding and lacing, preceded by some cutting and sewing, are the only skills needed.
* Recycling used goods into a new and useful form saves both our personal pocketbooks and the energy expenditure of the larger community.
* The rugs fit well into any room — kitchen, bedroom, living room, den, dining room, hallway — even stairway.
* Easily cleaned and reversible, braided rugs are simple to mend or even to enlarge if necessary.
* While there's no denying that a braided rug takes time to complete, the work is easily done in snatches of time and the rug can even be used and admired as it grows. Since there is no elaborate frame or equipment to set up, rug braiding makes good pick-up work.
* There will never be another rug quite like the one you create, from your own findings, for your own home.

*   As a cottage industry, producing braided rugs allows you to keep the homestead fires going, collect the eggs and weed the garden, while working on your craft at your own hours and your own pace. The rugs are in demand in many craft, antique, and specialty shops, in both cities and small towns.

The most important ingredient of a braided rug — outside of the care and craftsmanship that go into it — is the recycled fabric from which it's made. You'll want to use wool that has not been worn threadbare, of course, or your finished product won't be worth your time or (if you sell it) the buyer's money. Woolen fabric — or a blend of wool and acrylic or other man-made fiber — is the best choice. Synthetics lack that springy, alive quality and cotton — while attractive — is stiff to work with and quick to wear out.

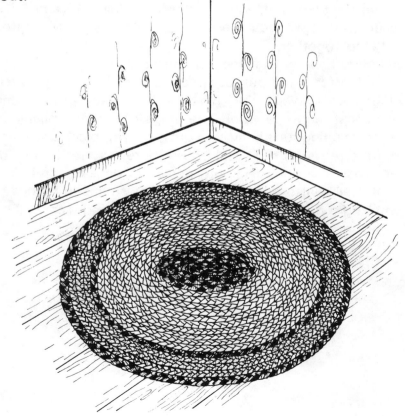

Fabrics to Avoid

Plenty of woolen garments are discarded for reasons that have nothing to do with the amount of wear left in them, however. You can usually afford to be discriminating in your choice of fabric.

For example, you will want to avoid:

1. Open, coarsely woven fabric that is likely to ravel and show wear on the individual threads.

2. Threadbare fabrics (but if only elbows or knees are worn on an otherwise sound piece of clothing, you can cut out the weak spots and use the rest).

3. Garments with many seams: a many-gored skirt or highly styled jacket with many darts and short sections of fabric sewn together. This is a matter of individual preference, though; if the garment is free, the fabric is good, and you have plenty of time, you may not mind doing the extensive piecing that will be necessary to join many short lengths of wool together.

4. Hard-finish wool fabric from men's suits — although unsuitable for some purposes, it is useful for others. Such fabric wears well if the entire rug is made from the same thin, flat, nap-free wool. The range of colors available in men's suiting runs heavily to grey, brown, black and blue, so the resulting rug would have more texture than color interest. The one thing you should not do is to combine a flat, hard-finish wool fabric with softer napped fabrics in making a rug. The braid will be crooked and wear will be uneven.

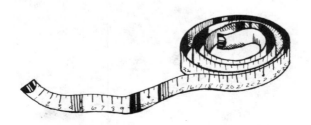

The Best Garments

Many kinds of discarded clothing can be valuable braided rug ingredients. . .old wool bathrobes (especially good because they yield nice long strips), out-of-style coats, torn slacks, moth-eaten blankets, a skirt that shrank or a wool dress that no longer fits. If you ask around a bit, especially at fall and spring cleaning times, you'll probably find that friends and relatives have usable discards that will give you a good start for your rug.

After you've raided all available attics, you may want to build up your collection of rug wool further by shopping at rummage sales and thrift shops — always good sources for used clothing at reasonable and often extremely low-prices. (Hint: try on some of your best finds. Perhaps you'll want to wear them for a while before cutting them up!)

Many rug makers routinely wash clothing purchased at such sales. The easiest way to do this is to run a load of the wool garments through your washing machine. Hot water and rapid agitation usually cause some shrinkage, but that only serves to tighten the weave of the fabric and detracts in no way from its usability in the rug.

Try Dyeing

If you find white wool fabric, you may want to try dyeing it a color that is difficult to find otherwise, using either commercial dye or natural colorings such as black walnut shells or onion skins.

Strips and yardage of new wool fabric may be purchased, usually by the pound, at mill end stores and factory outlets. A rug made entirely of such new wool will be more expensive than one made of found materials and recycled clothing, but it will still be a good value, a creative satisfaction to make, and a design unlike any other. It is perfectly all right to mix new wool and used wool, as long as the weight and nap of the fabrics are reasonably well matched.

Supplies You Need

The other supplies you'll need, in addition to the wool fabric, are basic hand sewing supplies found in most households or easily purchased if not readily at hand:

1. Sharp sewing scissors.

2. Thread:
    a. Heavy duty for piecing strips.
    b. Button and carpet thread for lacing braids together.
    Note: do not use nylon thread to lace together wool braids. The nylon may cut through the wool in time, as the rug wears.

3. Bodkin-a flat, blunt "poker" used to lace the braids together.

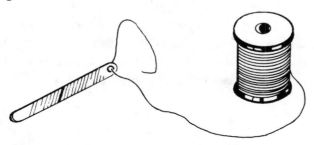

4. Knife or seam ripper.

5. Tape measure or yardstick.

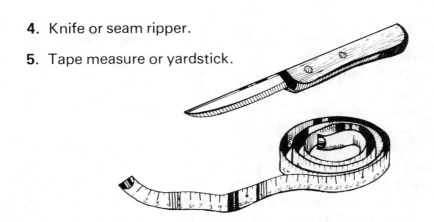

   With these materials assembled, all you need in order to create a rug is some time and the skill of your hands, which will grow as you work with the braids and shape them into the rug you have in mind. The difference between a pleasing finished product and a poor one lies in craftsmanship. . . in that attention to detail and that oneness with the materials that produces the proper yank on the thread and the controlled pull on the braid. You'll get the feel of this as you proceed. It's a good idea to make your first rug a small one; you can always enlarge it later.

How to Begin

   First, prepare your wool strips for braiding by cutting up the clothes and yard goods you've collected. You'll be able to salvage most of the wool if you'll rip the seams open. If you have the time and patience to do the necessary extra piecing, you can even use the collars and other short sections. Intersperse the short strips with longer ones in sewing them together, though, to avoid undue extra bulk in the braid from too many piecing seams placed close together.

Recycle the wool scraps that are too small for anything else by soaking them thoroughly with water and burying them in the garden or compost pile. Keep an eye out too, while ripping up the clothing, for reusable zippers, coat linings and buttons. And check the pockets. . .they've been known to contain coins!

Next, cut or tear the wool into strips. Some heavy fabrics don't tear readily and must be cut. To tear light and medium weight wool, cut three-inch notches all along the short edge and then tear off the strips one by one. Children often enjoy doing this job. If the fabric has an accumulation of dust and lint in the seams, you might want to do your tearing outdoors.

Width Varies

The width of the strips varies with the weight of the fabric. Cut the heavier woolens into strips two inches wide. (Never less, or the raw edges will not stay rolled in.) Use a three-inch width for lighter weight fabrics that require more self-padding as they're folded together. Don't cut strips any wider than three inches; any fabric that needs that much self-padding is not heavy enough for your rug.

These strips of fabric must be sewn together to make a continuous length which will form one-third of the braid. You can sew together all of the strips of one kind of fabric before starting the rug if you wish, but you will find that you have a lot of untangling to do as you braid. It is simpler to sew together only a few strips at a time. Keep the strips together by rolling them into a wheel, fastening the last loose strip with a pin. Then, when you come to a break in the continuity of the strip as you use up the wheel of wool, you can join the cut ends with hand stitches.

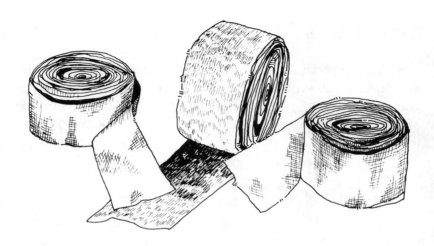

Sort the Colors

As you accumulate wheels of the prepared strips, it's a good idea to sort the colors, at least into rough categories. Quite likely you'll find that you have a quantity of grey, blue, and black wheels, a fair number of reds and brown-tan tones, and a smaller number of greens, orange-yellow-golds, pinks, lavenders, turquoises, maroons, and whites. Plaids may be either kept together or grouped by their predominating color, along with the rolls of plain colors. You may want to keep a special category for certain rich or subtle shades that you wish to use to best advantage. Many rug braiders use their more hard-to-find colors to make the initial strip of the rug in order to achieve the greatest impact from the limited amount of wool available in the unusual shades.

For example, if you want a gold accent in your rug, but have only one small roll of gold strips, start the rug with the gold, braided with two other strips of a more plentiful color, continue the main body of your rug with the colors you have abundantly available, and use a single strand of gold once again, about 10- 12 inches (depending on rug size) before finishing off the rug.

Sew on Bias

Strips are always sewn together on the bias. . .that is, at an angle. If you were to sew them straight across the ends, you would have a bulky, hard-to-manage lump to braid around. The diagonal seam distributes the bulk and keeps the braid pliable.

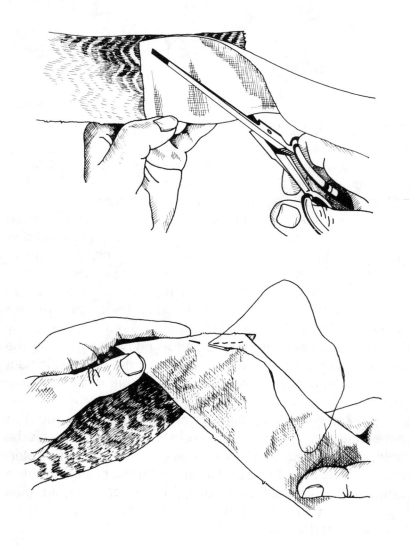

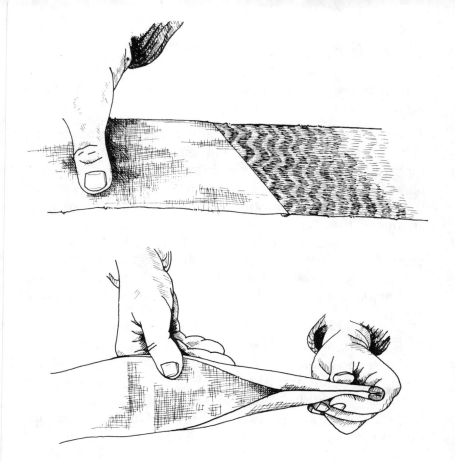

It is not difficult to find the true bias of the fabric you're working with. The bias runs diagonally at a 45° angle across the straight-of-the-goods. To make a true bias cut, overlap the two strips to be joined — right sides up — for as many inches as they are wide (two-inch overlap for two-inch wide strips, for example) and cut diagonally across the double layer of fabric from one corner to the other. Then, with the right sides facing, line up the newly cut edges at right angles and sew them firmly together, using either a tight machine stitch or a back-hand stitch by hand. Use double thread, preferably heavy-duty, for hand stitching. It isn't necessary to match the thread color to the wool exactly, but avoid, for example, black thread to piece a very light colored strip.

Color Options

In planning the color scheme of your rug, you have several options.

1. Hit-or-miss, the method used in most very old rugs, involves braiding in colors at random as they come. For a more refined version of hit-and-miss which many people find pleasing, carry a uniform strand of a basic color such as grey, tan or black throughout the rug, mixing in other shades as they become available. Hit-or-miss rugs are delightfully informal and versatile. The method is a good choice for a person who must build up a stockpile of wool slowly, as well as for one who simply wants to try the technique without being committed to a definite color scheme.

2. Basic monotone — a relatively neutral rug made by braiding together shades of brown and tan, grey with a color, or of blue and navy. Such a rug requires a sizable accumulation of the right colors of wool. It is less interesting, perhaps, to work on than a more highly colored rug, but in many cases it might be just the right touch for a certain room.

3. Contrasting colors.
Some attractive combinations are:

> Brown, gold, and red
> Red, white, black and grey
> Maroon, pink and grey
> Green, navy and grey
> Red, grey, blue, and green
> Orange, green, brown, and tan.

The choice of colors is a matter of personal taste, availability and harmony with already existing home furnishings. There's no right or wrong in color choice. If it pleases you, use it.

4. Ombre blends require careful planning and a good supply of the right colors. They can be stunning when well done. To make an ombre blend, choose varying tones and shades of a color you like — yellow, gold and orange or rust, brown, orange or pale pink, deep pink and maroon. You can either braid the three different tones together or shade from light to dark and back again. Including one neutral shade — grey, navy, black or tan where appropriate, perhaps as an occasional strand or whole strip, helps to set off the other colors. Not the best choice for your first project, but a satisfying achievement for the more experienced and well supplied rug braider.

Braid Aid

Beginners, attempting to create a plump and firm braid, often have difficulty in keeping the three strips properly folded. For them the Braid-Aid shown in these illustrations is a help — much like several extra fingers on each hand, with one aid holding each of the three tube-strips. More experienced braiders usually lay these aside, finding they can work more quickly without them.

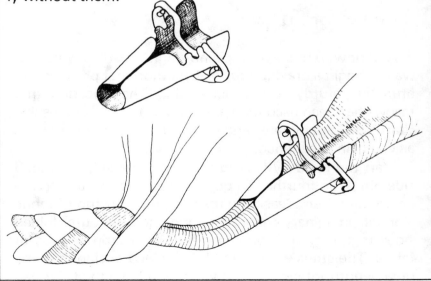

Subdued Colors

Most of the old braided rugs are done in subdued colors. Age has faded and softened whatever bright colors they might have had. Then too, the range of colors available to the traditional braided rug maker of old was limited. Some very old rugs contain fabrics that were hand dyed using native dye plants.

Even a little bit of red or yellow will liven up an otherwise dull rug. Plaids usually look best when braided with two solid color strips. A large amount of the same fabric may be used either to make several solid rounds of braid, or as one or two strands in a wider section of mixed braids. Try both methods to determine which you prefer for the rug you are making. A solid band of light-colored braid shows the dirt more readily than a mixture of colors. A solid band of navy, black or dark brown (depending on color scheme) around the perimeter of the rug makes an emphatic finishing touch that frames and enhances the mixed colors in the rug.

Time to Braid

And now to braid! There is no single, absolutely correct way to begin a braided rug. Any method that produces an attractive, sturdy result is acceptable. The procedure that follows has been used for many years with excellent results. Start here, at any rate, and work out your own variations as you gain experience.

Start the braid by folding each of three strips — good side out — in fourths. To do this, fold each side in to the center and then crease the resulting double strip of fabric along its imaginary center line, bringing both outer folded sides together, and forming a four-layer strip or tube of fabric. The strips will not hold this folded position for any great length, of course, but when you have them formed correctly from the beginning, they are headed in the right direction when they come to your hand and you will find that you can smooth and control the folds easily as you braid.

Starting the Braid

There are several acceptable ways to start the braid. The old country way, which I learned first, is to place the three four-ply strips on top of each other and sew them together across the cut ends.

Another, more polished method covers all the raw edges.

Suppose you are beginning your rug with three colors. Sew a strip of color A to a strip of color B in a bias seam as described (call this strip AB).

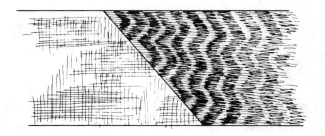

Fold color C into a four-ply tube-strip with raw edges inside.

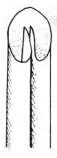

Fold raw edges of strip AB in to meet at center of strip.

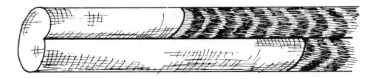

Insert raw edge of folded strip C at seam joining colors A and B and sew firmly in place.

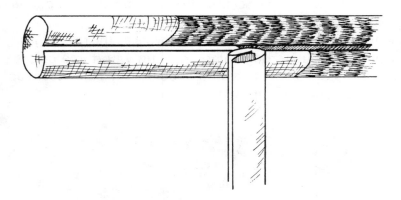

Fold top half of strip AB down to cover raw edges of strip C. You now have a "T" with color C sandwiched between layers 1 and 2, and 3 and 4, of strip AB.

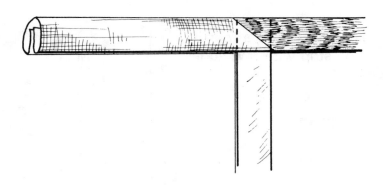

Flat Edges

No matter which way you choose to start the braid, the process of braiding is the same. Start braiding just as you would braid hair or yarn, except that you must take extra care to fold the strips around to make flat rather than twisted edges. Braiding is simple, but in case you don't know how, study the illustration, and you'll quickly learn. If you are learning, it is easier to work with three different colors.

Put 3 over 2 toward the left.

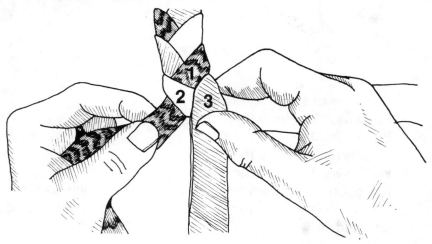

Put 1 over 3 toward the right.

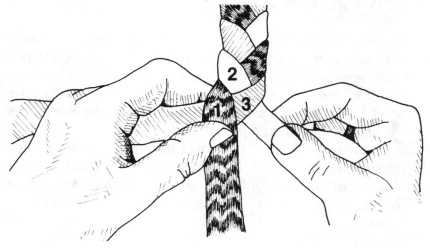

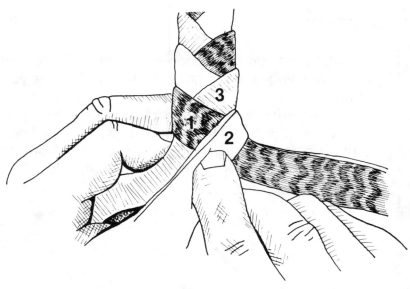

Put 2 over 1 toward the left.
Put 3 over 2 toward the right.
Put 1 over 3 toward the left.
Put 2 over 1 toward the right.
Put 3 over 2 toward the left, etc.

It is good to try this a few times, even if you have braided other materials before, to practice getting a tight, plump and even braid.

Tension Needed

When starting the rug, for the first few feet, the braid will seem to be everywhere and nowhere. You need to put some tension on it in order to get an even braid. Pin, tie or clamp it — or close a window or drawer on the end of the braid — so that you can pull on it gently as you work. This will help to keep it straight and even.

Braid about two or three yards before beginning to lace the rug together. For a hit-or-miss rug in which color planning is not critical, you could let your braid accumulate a bit longer, but not too long, or it will be tangled and unruly when you try to form the rug. In a highly structured rug with a very exact color plan, you will want to braid and lace alternatively at short, regular intervals so that you can tell when it is time to change colors.

What Length?

How do you determine the proper length for your starting braid? Simple mathematics. The projected length of the rug minus its projected width equals the length of the starting braid. For a 7' × 9' rug, then, you would plan on an initial center braid two feet in length. Allow a few extra inches, say about three inches for every two feet of the starting braid, to make up for the slight shrinkage effect caused by lacing the braids together. Thus, for a 7' × 9' rug, you would measure out an actual 2' 3" for your center braid.

Double the Braid Back

Mark the end of the starting length of braid with a safety pin, and double the braid back on itself at this point, so that you have two rows of braids side by side. Force both sections of the braid to lie flat as you form this rounded corner. When lacing a rug together, always lay your work on a hard, flat surface.

Thread your bodkin (a blunt needle) with a double strand of heavy button-and-carpet thread about a yard long. Using a longer thread won't save any time and it is almost sure to tangle. Knot the end of the thread and, starting at the pin-marked corner, poke the bodkin *between* the braid folds. Take several stitches to secure the thread and then begin to lace by inserting the bodkin through every other braid fold, alternating from left to right. Pull firmly with your right hand as you hold the braids flat with your left.

At no time should the bodkin pierce the fabric. It always

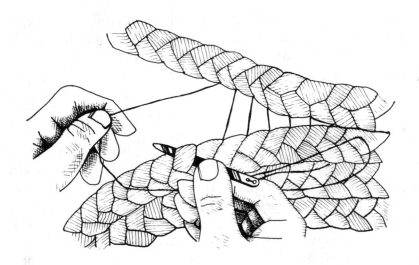

leads the thread *between* the folds of fabric. This is what makes the rug reversible.

When you have laced your first length of braid down to the turning point, you will begin to see where craftsmanship comes into play. If you sew too tightly around corners, your rug will not lie flat; too loosely, and the rounds will gap unattractively. Rounding the corners on a braided rug requires judgment and common sense; there are no hard-and-fast rules, just guidelines. Loops on the sewn-on braid should match loops on the rug. As you hold that first braid around the corners, you can see what needs to happen.

To Keep It Flat

For the first six to ten rounds — *at the corners only* — the stitches on the body of the rug must be closer together than those on the braid you're attaching. So after lacing through a loop on the outer braid, and then through the next loop on the body of the rug, you then *skip* a loop on the outer braid and lace the following loop to the *very next* loop on the body of the rug. (Skip a loop on the new braid; don't skip on the rug body.)

In this way, you "hold back" the attaching braid so that it stays flat. Too many of these double stitches, though, will cause the rug to ripple rather than buckle. Later, as the project grows and the turns are less sharp, you won't need to hold back the outside braid as often in order to match the loops, as you had to during the first few rounds. The process soon becomes second nature. That old folk saying seems to be true here: "Well begun is half done."

For a round rug, of course, there's no need to compute the length of a starting braid. Just snail the braid around and around as you hold if flat and continually correct for the increasing by making the "skip" stitches every few inches in the beginning, and only each foot or so as the rug enlarges.

Other Designs

The designs of braided rugs can reflect the creativity of the braider. Here are three ideas.

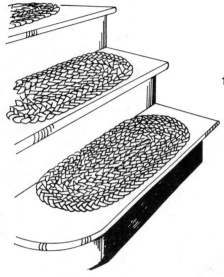

The stair tread, explained in text of bulletin.

The chain, two or more circles sewn together, then enclosed with three or more braids. Good for a runner.

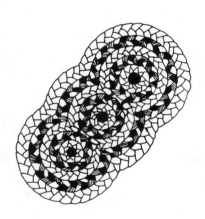

Ideal for a fireplace front is this half-circle, made, not of one long braid, but a series of increasingly longer ones.

Start Over

If it ever appears that your rug is buckling or rippling, you lose nothing but time by unlacing the piece and starting again from shortly before the point where it begins to look misshapen. Even the thread can be used again. Ripping out completed work may be painful but the results are worth it.

Dimples or folds in the braids are the result of using uneven tension in braiding or combining fabrics of varied weight, or of folding the strips unevenly.

Whenever you join on a new lacing thread, tie it to the old one on a firm knot, leaving ¾" ends which can be tucked back between the loops.

Completing The Rug

Complete the rug by tapering the last 6"-8" of the braid. To do this, trim each strip so that it tapers to about half its original width at the cut end. Braid these narrow ends, carefully rolling in the edges, and lace the tapered butt firmly to the rug, retracing the last few lacing stitches for extra firmness. Leave a 2"-3" length of the lacing thread and weave it back between the braids, using a crochet hook, to form a secure, invisible ending.

Square Rugs

In addition to the traditional round and oval forms, rugs may be braided in squares and in long straight mats for stair or hallway carpeting. To make square or rectangular rugs, compute the length of the center strip as you would for an oval rug. In place of the gradual increases made at the shoulders of the rounded rugs, the squared-off rugs are laced straight down each side, with an extra fold made in the braid at the point where it turns the corner, forming an L-joint that gives the rug its squared-off shape. Skip the loop at the point of the corner when lacing the rug together.

A runner or stair carpet may be made by lacing together parallel braids. In planning the length of such a rug, allow at least one inch per foot of shrinkage in the laced rug, and be sure to figure in any additional length needed to go around the lip of each stair tread.

Don't Hurry

There's no point in pretending that braided rugs can be made quickly. They can't. But nothing in the procedure requires your total concentration, either. You can open seams and rip strips while hearing homework lessons, enjoying a winter fire or herding the goats on their daily browse. Sewing, braiding and lacing can all be done in a leisurely way while visiting with friends, listening to music or practicing (some) yoga postures. But perhaps we try too much to make every minute doubly productive. The rhythm of the creative process is soothing and relaxing, reason enough for pursuing it.

Still, because a rug in progress can be left right on the floor where it's easy to work on, it will grow surprisingly fast. Perhaps your family and friends will want to add to your braid. Out-of-pocket investment for such a useful product is small, and even that small amount may be stretched out gradually as the rug progresses. In the end, you may well find that you enjoy the process of rug making as much as you enjoy having a completed rug. Then, of course, it's time to begin another!